snoopy's
facts & fun book about seasons

ABRIDGED EDITION

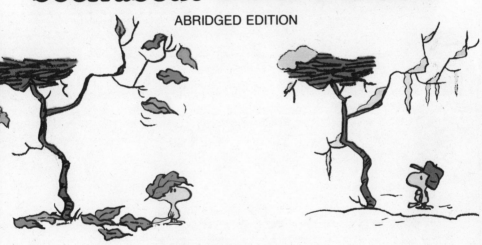

**Based on the
Charles M. Schulz Characters**

Happy House Books

Designed by Terry Flanagan

In spring the weather starts to get warm.
Trees have buds that will turn into new
green leaves.

Spring is the time
to plant seeds. The
seeds sprout into
little plants.

Sunshine and rain
help the plants grow
bigger... and bigger.

A windy day is just right for flying kites.

Spring is the beginning of baseball season.
Bring out the balls and bats and gloves
and—Play Ball!

When the weather gets very hot, summertime is here! Leaves are green, and flowers are in full bloom.

People go on vacation.

Some like to hike and camp in the woods.

When the weather starts to get cool, the leaves change colors. Autumn has come!
Soon the leaves fall off the trees. Raking leaves is fun!

It's time to go back to school.

On Halloween, children dress in scary costumes. Trick or treat!

Autumn is harvest time. Farmers bring in their crops.

Long ago, on Thanksgiving, people cele-
brated a good harvest. Today we give thanks
for our food, homes, family, and friends.

Autumn is football season. Go, team, go!

In the autumn many birds fly south to find
a warm place to live for the winter.

Winter weather is very cold. Everyone
dresses warmly.

A cold winter evening is a good time to sit
by the fire and drink hot chocolate.

At Christmas time, carolers go from door
to door singing Christmas songs.

At last the snow begins to melt. Birds
come back from their winter homes.
Spring is here again!